LEVEL
1
Jane
Goodall
Barbara Kramer
NATIONAL
GEOGRAPHIC
KiDS
New York

For kids who dream of great adventures —B.K.

For Jane: a pioneer, leader, and inspiration to generations of animal lovers —Team NGK

Random House Children's Books
A division of Penguin Random House LLC
1745 Broadway, New York, NY 10019
penguinrandomhouse.com
rhcbooks.com

Designed by Gustavo Tello and Eva Absher-Schantz

Author's Note
When Jane Goodall began studying chimpanzees, the way many researchers learned how animals acted in the wild was to go to where they lived and get close to them. Today, many scientists prefer to study animals from a distance with the help of technology such as motion-activated cameras and satellites. Goodall and other scientists came to agree that this approach makes the research safer for humans and does not disturb the animals. You may see older photos of Goodall up close with chimpanzees, but she later felt that contact between animals and humans was not a good idea. For that reason, in this book there are no photos of Goodall touching chimpanzees.

The publisher would like to thank Jane Goodall and the Jane Goodall Institute for contributing special photos and providing expert review; Mariam Jean Dreher, literacy reviewer; and Michelle Harris, fact-checker. Book team: Vivian Suchman, editorial director; Lori Epstein, senior director of photography; Lauren Sciortino, production design associate; Molly Reid, senior copy editor.

Library of Congress Cataloging-in-Publication Data is available upon request.

ISBN: 978-1-4262-2506-2 (trade paperback)
ISBN: 978-1-4262-2507-9 (lib. bdg.)

Manufactured in the United States of America
10 9 8 7 6 5 4 3 2 1

The authorized representative in the EU for product safety and compliance is Penguin Random House Ireland, Morrison Chambers, 32 Nassau Street, Dublin D02 YH68, Ireland, https://eu-contact.penguin.ie.

Random House Children's Books supports the First Amendment and celebrates the right to read.

Photo Credits
Abbreviations: AP = Alamy Stock Photo; AS = Adobe Stock; GI = Getty Images; JGI = Jane Goodall Institute; NGIC = National Geographic Image Collection

Cover: (Jane Goodall), CBS via GI; (chimpanzee), Fiona Rogers/Minden Pictures; 1, Hugo Van Lawick/NGIC; 3, Eric Issele/AS; 5, Hugo van Lawick/JGI; 6, Courtesy of the Goodall Family/JGI; 7, Courtesy of the Goodall Family/JGI; 8 (UP), thieury/AS; 8 (LO), George F. Mobley/NGIC; 9, Courtesy of the Goodall Family/JGI; 10, Library of Congress; 11, © Twentieth Century Fox Film Corporation/AP; 12 (UP), Imperial War Museums via GI; 12 (LO), studiovin/Shutterstock; 13 (UP), Wolverhampton City Council/Arts and Heritage/AP; 13 (CTR), sevaljevic/AS; 13 (LO), London Express/GI; 14, Courtesy of the Goodall Family/JGI; 15 (UP), George F. Mobley/NGIC; 15 (LO), Joan Travis/JGI; 16, Robert Sisson/NGIC; 17, Abeselom Zerit/AS; 18, Judy Goodall/JGI; 19, Jane Goodall/NGIC; 20, James/AS; 21, Hugo Van Lawick/NGIC; 22 (INSET), Hugo Van Lawick/NGIC; 22, George F. Mobley/NGIC; 23, Nathaniel Noir/AP; 24 (UP), Courtesy of the Goodall Family/JGI; 24 (LO LE), Jonny White/AP; 24 (LO RT), JGI; 25 (UP), Michael Nichols/NGIC; 25 (CTR), PixelPro/Alamy Stock; 25 (LO), Michael Nichols/NGIC; 26, Jens Schlueter/DDP/AFP via GI; 27, Brennan Linsley/AP Photo; 28 (LE), Martin Harvey/Photodisc/GI; 28 (RT), George F. Mobley/NGIC; 29 (UP LE), Courtesy of the Goodall Family/JGI; 29 (UP RT), Jane Goodall/JGI; 29 (CTR LE), Hugo Van Lawick/NGIC; 29 (CTR RT), Jeremy Piper/Newspix/GI; 29 (LO LE), Andrew Francis Wallace/Toronto Star via GI; 29 (LO RT), Ken Cedeno/Reuters; 31 (UP LE), © Twentieth Century Fox Film Corporation/AP; 31 (UP RT), Hugo Van Lawick/NGIC; 31 (LO LE), thieury/AS; 31 (LO RT), Hugo Van Lawick/NGIC; 32 (UP LE), Hugo Van Lawick/NGIC; 32 (UP RT), busaryev/AS; 32 (LO LE), FloridaStock/Shutterstock; 32 (LO RT), witsawat/AS

Table of Contents

Who Was Jane Goodall? 4

A Love for Animals 6

A Dream Begins 10

In Her Time 12

Going to Africa 14

New Ideas 20

6 Cool Facts
About Jane Goodall 24

Saving the Chimps 26

Goodall's Legacy 28

Picture Perfect 30

Glossary 32

Who Was Jane Goodall?

Jane Goodall was famous for studying chimpanzees. Some scientists study animals in labs or zoos. But Goodall went into the forest where the chimps lived.

She showed us what chimpanzees are like in the wild. She also taught us to keep animals safe.

Word to Know

CHIMPANZEE: An ape, up to five feet tall, that lives in the forests of Africa

Jane Goodall used binoculars to look at chimps from behind trees and bushes.

A Love for Animals

baby Jane with her toy chimp, Jubilee

Goodall was born on April 3, 1934, in London, England. Her family later moved to the town of Bournemouth (BORN-muth).

Goodall loved animals. She wanted to know all about them. She wondered, How do chickens lay eggs?

young Jane with her mother

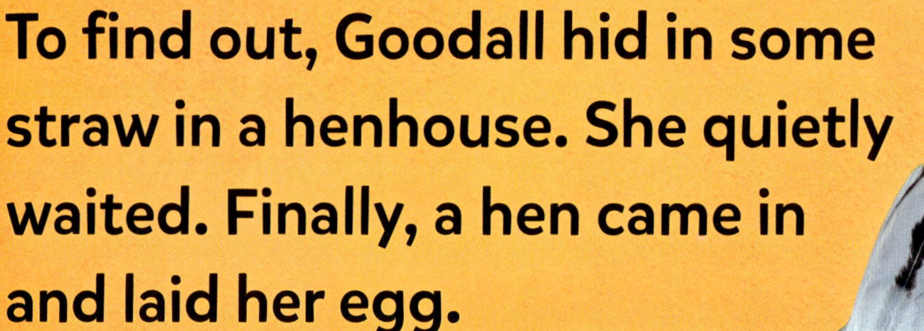

To find out, Goodall hid in some straw in a henhouse. She quietly waited. Finally, a hen came in and laid her egg.

Goodall was only five years old when she found out how chickens lay eggs.

In Her Own Words

"You have to be patient if you want to learn about animals."

young Jane feeding a pigeon

Goodall had her answer. But she had been gone for hours! Her mother was looking everywhere for her.

A Dream Begins

When Goodall was eight, she read *The Story of Doctor Dolittle.* This book is a made-up story about a doctor who goes to Africa. He can talk to animals. Goodall wanted to go to Africa to work with animals in real life.

As a child, Goodall read this book over and over.

The 1998 movie ***Dr. Doolittle*** **is about a doctor who can talk to animals.**

In Her Time

Goodall grew up in England in the early 1940s. What was life like for her back then?

World Events

England and other countries were fighting in World War II. Goodall's father went off to fight in the war.

School

Goodall took a bus each day to an all-girls' school. Some students lived at the school.

Getting Around

Gas was needed for fighting the war. Most people could not buy gas for their cars. They rode bikes or took buses instead.

Having Fun

There was no TV service during the war. People listened to the radio or went to the movies.

Jobs

After high school, some women worked in offices or became nurses or teachers. But not many became scientists.

Going to Africa

After high school, Goodall trained to be a secretary. She worked and saved her money.

AFRICA

Goodall and her friend Rusty

By 1957, she had enough for a trip to Africa. There, she met a scientist named Dr. Louis Leakey (LOO-us LEE-kee). He studied how early humans lived. He hired Goodall to be his secretary.

In Her Own Words

"My mother used to say to me if you really want something, you have to work hard, take advantage of opportunity, and never give up."

Goodall and Dr. Louis Leakey

Leakey searched for fossils and bones to learn more about early humans.

Leakey was looking for someone to study chimpanzees. He thought learning about chimps would help him learn more about early humans. This was just what Goodall wanted to do. But first, Leakey needed to raise money for the project.

While she waited for Leakey to raise the money, Goodall worked at a zoo in London. In 1960, she went back to Africa to begin her work. She set up a camp in the forest to study chimps where they lived. Each day, she looked for chimps. But they ran away and hid.

Goodall outside her tent in Gombe Stream National Park in Tanzania

Goodall looking for chimpanzees

New Ideas

Months later, some chimps let Goodall get closer. One day, she saw a chimp rip leaves off a stick. He poked it into a hole, and then pulled it out. The stick was covered with termites. He gobbled them up! Until then, many scientists thought only humans knew how to make tools.

Word to Know

TERMITE: A small, ant-like insect that lives in groups and eats wood

A chimpanzee uses a blade of grass as a tool to get termites.

In Her Own Words

"We are not the only beings on the planet with personalities, thoughts, and—most importantly—feelings."

Goodall also learned chimpanzees had feelings. They showed love, joy, and anger—just like people.

At the end of 1961, Goodall went back to England to go to college. She learned more about how animals act. In 1965, she earned a doctorate. Now she was Dr. Goodall.

Word to Know

DOCTORATE: The highest degree a student can earn from a college

Goodall went to Newnham College at the University of Cambridge.

6 Cool Facts About Jane Goodall

1 Goodall rode on a horse for the **first time** when she was **two years old.** She began taking riding lessons when she was about 11.

2 Goodall wrote more than **25 books** about chimpanzees and her work.

3 When she was **12 years old,** Goodall **started a nature club.** It was called the **Alligator Club.**

4

Goodall **kept** her childhood toy, **Jubilee.** But he went bald from so much loving.

5

When Goodall spoke to large groups, she **liked to welcome** them with a **chimpanzee call.**

6

Goodall saw that **chimps** were all **different and special,** just like humans. So she **gave them names.** Other scientists gave them numbers.

Saving the Chimps

In 1977, Goodall created the Jane Goodall Institute to carry on her work. She soon learned chimpanzees could become endangered. She wanted to help them.

Goodall also helped chimpanzees in zoos.

Word to Know

ENDANGERED: At risk of dying out

Goodall believed that everyone could help. In 1991, Goodall started a program called Roots & Shoots. It helps kids create projects that support people, animals, and nature.

Goodall's Legacy

Goodall died in 2025. She lived to be 91. Before she died, she was given the U.S. Presidential Medal of Freedom. Today, many people carry on her work to take care of our planet.

In Her Own Words

"Every individual has a role to play. Every individual makes a difference."

1934
Born on April 3

1957
Takes her first trip to Africa

1960
Begins her study of chimpanzees

1965
Earns her doctorate

1977
Creates the Jane Goodall Institute

1991
Starts the Roots & Shoots program

2002
Becomes a UN Messenger of Peace

2025
Dies on October 1

Picture Perfect

The sentences below tell things about Jane Goodall's life. Can you find the perfect picture for each one? Answers are on page 31.

1. Goodall saw chimpanzees make a tool to get a snack.
2. As a kid, Goodall hid in some straw to find out how eggs were laid.
3. Goodall studied chimpanzees where they lived.
4. This made-up person talks to animals, but Goodall wanted to work with animals in real life.

Answers: 1. B; 2. C; 3. D; 4. A

Glossary

Chimpanzee

An ape, up to five feet tall, that lives in the forests of Africa

Doctorate

The highest degree a student can earn from a college

Endangered

At risk of dying out

Termite

A small, ant-like insect that lives in groups and eats wood

National Geographic Kids Readers

for curious kids at every reading level!

Pre-reader • **Ready to read**

Level 1 Co-reader • **Starting to read together**

Starting to read

Level 1 books are just right for kids who are beginning to read on their own.

Level 2 • **Reading independently**

Level 3 • **Fluent reader**

Manufactured in the United States of America

rhcbooks.com | @randomhousekids

US $5.99 / $7.99 CAN

ISBN 978-1-4262-2506-2